Evaluation of the Sensitivity of Inventory and Monitoring National Parks to Nutrient Enrichment Effects from Atmospheric Nitrogen Deposition

Appalachian Highlands Network (APHN)

Natural Resource Report NPS/NRPC/ARD/NRR—2011/302

T. J. Sullivan
T. C. McDonnell
G. T. McPherson
S. D. Mackey
D. Moore

E&S Environmental Chemistry, Inc.
P.O. Box 609
Corvallis, OR 97339

February 2011

U.S. Department of the Interior
National Park Service
Natural Resource Program Center
Denver, Colorado

The National Park Service, Natural Resource Program Center publishes a range of reports that address natural resource topics of interest and applicability to a broad audience in the National Park Service and others in natural resource management, including scientists, conservation and environmental constituencies, and the public.

The Natural Resource Report Series is used to disseminate high-priority, current natural resource management information with managerial application. The series targets a general, diverse audience, and may contain NPS policy considerations or address sensitive issues of management applicability.

All manuscripts in the series receive the appropriate level of peer review to ensure that the information is scientifically credible, technically accurate, appropriately written for the intended audience, and designed and published in a professional manner.

This report received peer review by subject-matter experts who were not directly involved in the collection, analysis, or reporting of the data. Data in this report were collected and analyzed using methods based on established, peer-reviewed protocols and were analyzed and interpreted within the guidelines of the protocols.

This report is available from Air Resources Division of the NPS (http://www.nature.nps.gov/air/Permits/ARIS/networks/n-sensitivity.cfm) and the Natural Resource Publications Management website (http://www.nature.nps.gov/publications/nrpm/)

Please cite this publication as:

Sullivan, T. J., T. C. McDonnell, G. T. McPherson, S. D. Mackey, and D. Moore. 2011. Evaluation of the sensitivity of inventory and monitoring national parks to nutrient enrichment effects from atmospheric nitrogen deposition: Appalachian Highlands Network (APHN). Natural Resource Report NPS/NRPC/ARD/NRR—2011/302. National Park Service, Denver, Colorado.

NPS 910/106632, February 2011

Appalachian Highlands Network (APHN)

National maps of atmospheric N emissions and deposition are provided in Maps A and B as context for subsequent network data presentations. Map A shows county level emissions of total N for the year 2002. Map B shows total N deposition, again for the year 2002.

The Appalachian Highlands Network contains three parks that are larger than 100 square miles: Great Smoky Mountains (GRSM), Big South Fork (BISO), and Blue Ridge (BLRI). It also contains one smaller park: Obed (OBRI).

Total N emissions, by county, are shown in Map C for lands in and surrounding the Appalachian Highlands Network. County-level annual emissions within the network ranged from less than 1 ton per square mile to greater than 100 tons per square mile. In general, annual emissions from most counties were between 1 and 20 tons per square mile. Individual point source emissions of oxidized (nitrogen oxides, NO_x) and reduced (ammonia, NH_3) N are shown in Map D. All large (larger than 1,000 tons per year) N point sources within the network, and most large point sources near the network, were oxidized N sources. Only one large point source of reduced N was located in proximity to the network; it was in Virginia, generally to the northeast of the network. There were two large point sources of NO_x within the network in Tennessee, situated between GRSM and BISO; each emitted more than 4,000 tons per year of oxidized N. Many other relatively large point sources of oxidized N occur in the vicinity of the network boundaries. Urban centers within the network and within a 300 mile buffer around the network are shown in Map E. Few human population centers of any magnitude are found in this network.

Total N deposition in and around the network is shown in Map F. Included in this analysis are both wet and dry forms of N deposition and both the oxidized and reduced N species. Total N deposition within the network ranged from as low as 2 to 5 kg N/ha/yr per year to as high as 10 to 15 kg N/ha/yr. In addition, it is known that cloud deposition, which is not represented in the total deposition values depicted on the map, can be quite high at high-elevation sites (especially higher than 1,500 m) that occur in and around GRSM. At the highest elevation locations, the total N deposition, including cloud inputs, might be as much as double the wet plus dry deposition values that are mapped from NADP interpolations and CMAQ simulations in Map F.

Land cover in and around the network is shown in Map G. The predominant cover types within this network are generally forest and pasture/hay. Land cover within the major parks that occur in this network is primarily forested.

Map H, which shows the distribution within the larger parks that occur in a network of the five vegetation types thought to be most responsive to nutrient N enrichment effects (arctic, alpine, grassland and meadow, wetland, and arid and semi-arid), is not shown for this network. The vegetation types thought to be most sensitive to nutrient N enrichment are generally not found in the principal parks that occur within this network (GRSM and BISO), other than small amounts of wetland and grassland and meadow which are not evident at the map scale of the entire parks or the entire network. Although some of the forests in GRSM are considered sensitive to acidification and associated N-saturation (presented in a separate analysis), the forest vegetation is not considered especially sensitive to nutrient enrichment impacts from atmospheric N deposition.

Park lands requiring special protection against potential adverse impacts associated with nutrient N enrichment from atmospheric N deposition are shown on Map I. The land designations used to identify this heightened protection included Class I designation under the CAAA and wilderness designation. Also shown on Map I are all federal lands designated as wilderness, both lands managed by NPS and also lands managed by other federal agencies. GRSM is designated as a Class I area. There are also substantial areas scattered throughout the network that are designated as wilderness.

High elevation lakes might be more prone than lakes at lower elevation to N-limitation, and therefore are considered potentially more susceptible to eutrophication in response to atmospheric N input. As shown on Map J, there are lakes along the boundary of this park. In addition, elevations in GRSM are among the highest in the eastern United States, with the majority of the park lands being higher than 1,000 m elevation. Nevertheless, lakes within GRSM are generally not located at high elevation, and are therefore not considered to be especially sensitive to nutrient enrichment impacts.

Network rankings are given in Figures A through C as the average ranking of the Pollutant Exposure, Ecosystem Sensitivity, and Park Protection metrics, respectively. Figure D shows the overall network Summary Risk ranking. In each figure, the rank for this particular network is highlighted to show its relative position compared with the ranks of the other 31 networks.

The Appalachian Highlands Network is ranked Moderate in N Pollutant Exposure, at the top of the third quintile (coded yellow), among networks (Figure A). This ranking is likely biased low because it does not include cloud deposition, which is substantial at high elevations in and around GRSM. Nitrogen emissions within and upwind of the network and N deposition within the network are both moderately high. The Ecosystem Sensitivity ranking for APHN is Low, in the second lowest quintile among networks (Figure B). This is because vegetation is primarily forest, which is not expected to be especially sensitive to nutrient enrichment effects from N deposition compared with other vegetation types that are more common in other networks. In addition, there are few or no high-elevation lakes. Some forest types and some tree species, including some within this network, are known to be sensitive to acidification impacts, which can be caused by both N and sulfur deposition. These effects are addressed in a separate report. This network ranks in the third quintile in Park Protection (Figure C), having moderate amounts of protected lands.

In combination, the network rankings for Pollutant Exposure, Ecosystem Sensitivity, and Park Protection yield an overall Network Risk ranking that is moderately high, in the second highest quintile among all networks. The overall level of concern for nutrient N enrichment effects on I&M parks within this network is considered High.

Similarly, park rankings are given in Figures E through H for the same metrics. In the case of the park rankings, we only show in the figures the parks that are larger than 100 square miles. Relative ranks for all parks, including the smaller parks, are given in Table A and Appendix B. As for the network ranking figures, the park ranking figures highlight those parks that occur in this network to show their relative position compared with parks in the other 31 networks. Note that the rankings shown in Figures E through H reflect the rank of a given park compared with all other parks, irrespective of size.

Table A. Relative rankings of individual I&M parks within the network for Pollutant Exposure, Ecosystem Sensitivity, Park Protection, and overall Summary Risk from atmospheric nutrient N enrichment.

I&M Parks[2] in Network	Relative Ranking of Individual Parks[1]			
	Pollutant Exposure	Ecosystem Sensitivity	Park Protection	Summary Risk
Big South Fork	High	Very Low	Moderate	Low
Blue Ridge	High	Moderate	High	Very High
Great Smoky Mountains	High	Very Low	Very High	Very High
Obed	High	Very Low	Moderate	Low

[1] Relative park rankings are designated according to quintile ranking, among all I&M Parks, from the lowest quintile (very low risk) to the highest quintile (very high risk).
[2] Park names are printed in bold italic for parks larger than 100 square miles.

All four individual parks in this network (BLRI, GRSM, BISO, and OBRI) are ranked High in park-specific Pollutant Exposure (Table A, Figure E), indicating high levels of atmospheric nutrient N deposition. It is likely that GRSM should be ranked even higher because it is known to receive substantial cloud deposition of N, which is not included in the mapped rankings. In contrast, the Ecosystem Sensitivity ranking for each of these parks is lower (Figure F, Table A), mainly because the vegetation in these parks is largely forested, and there are few (three in BLRI) high-elevation lakes. The Park Protection ranking is High for BLRI and Very High for GRSM (Figure G), but only moderate in BISO and OBRI. The parks in this network show divergent results for overall Summary Risk ranking (Table A, Figure H). GRSM and BLRI rank within the top quintile; Summary Risk rankings for the other two parks are Low.

The Appalachian Trail (AT) corridor is not part of any particular network, but rather bisects a number of networks along its path between Maine and Georgia. We present data for the AT corridor here, as part of the Appalachian Highlands Network. Total N emissions within the counties adjacent to the AT corridor vary from less than 1 ton per square mile to more than 20 tons per square mile per year (Map AT-C). Large point sources of N in proximity to the AT are almost exclusively oxidized N sources (Map AT-D). Few large point sources are found adjacent to the AT north of New Jersey. To the south, however, there are many large NO_x point sources, both in close proximity to the corridor and in the Ohio River Valley to the west. Relatively large urban population centers (> 100,000 people) occur in relatively close proximity to the AT corridor along much of its length, with the exception of the northernmost portion in Maine (Map AT-E). The highest density of population centers along the corridor occurs between Boston and Washington DC. Total N deposition along the corridor is fairly low (2 to 5 kg N/ha/yr) in northern Maine, but is above 10 kg N/ha/yr along much of the corridor length between southern Vermont and southern Virginia (Map AT-F). Total N deposition is higher in and around GRSM than is shown on the map because of the importance of cloud deposition at very high elevation.

Most of the AT corridor is forested, especially in the north and in the south (Map AT-G). Substantial land areas classified as pasture/hay and some row crops and developed land occur in the middle section of the corridor. Because the AT follows ridgelines along much of its length, surface waters within the corridor tend to be primarily first and second order streams, rather than lakes. Although much of the trail location is forested, scattered meadows and wetlands also occur in some locations.

The AT corridor passes through Class I and wilderness areas, most notably within GRSM and Shenandoah National Park (SHEN; Map AT-I), both of which are classified as Class I. There are numerous wilderness areas scattered along the AT corridor, mainly along the northernmost section (in Vermont, New Hampshire, and Maine) and the southern section (in Virginia, North Carolina, Tennessee, and Georgia).

Map A.   National map of total N emissions by county for the year 2002. Both oxidized (nitrogen oxides, NO_x) and reduced (ammonia, NH_3) forms of N are included. The total is expressed in tons per square mile per year. (Source of data: EPA National Emissions Inventory, http://www.epa.gov/ttn/chief/net/2002inventory.html)

Map B.   Total N deposition for the conterminous United States for the year 2002, expressed in units of kilograms of N deposited from the atmosphere to the earth surface per hectare per year. Wet and dry forms of both oxidized (nitrogen oxides, NO_x) and reduced (ammonia, NH_3) N are included. For the eastern half of the country, wet deposition values were derived from interpolated measured values from NADP (three-year average centered on 2002) and dry deposition values were derived from 12-km CMAQ model projections for 2002. For the western half of the country, both wet and dry deposition values were derived from 36-km CMAQ model projections for 2002. NADP interpolations were performed using the approach of Grimm and Lynch (1997). CMAQ model projections were provided by Robin Dennis, U.S. EPA.

Map C.   Total N emissions by county for lands surrounding the network, expressed as tons of N emitted into the atmosphere per square mile per year. The total includes both oxidized (nitrogen oxides, NO_x) and reduced (ammonia, NH_3) N. (Source of data: EPA National Emissions Inventory, http://www.epa.gov/ttn/chief/net/2002inventory.html)

Map D.   Major point source emissions of oxidized (nitrogen oxides, NO_x) and reduced (ammonia, NH_3) N in and around the network. The base of each vertical bar is positioned in the map at the approximate location of the source. The height of the bar is proportional to the magnitude of the source. (Source of data: EPA National Emissions Inventory, http://www.epa.gov/ttn/chief/net/2002inventory.html)

Map E.   Urban centers having more than 10,000 people within the network and within a 300-mile buffer around the perimeter of the network. (Source of data: U.S. Census 2000)

Map F.   Total N deposition in and around the network. Included in the total are wet plus dry forms of both oxidized (nitrogen oxides, NO_x) and reduced (ammonia, NH_3) N. Values are expressed as kilograms of N deposited per hectare per year. (Source of data: Interpolated NADP wet and CMAQ Model dry deposition data for 2002; see information for Map B above for details)

Map G.   Land cover types in and around the network, based on the National Land Cover dataset. (Source of data: National Land Cover Dataset, http://www.mrlc.gov/nlcd_multizone_map.php)

Map I.   Lands within the network that are classified as Class I or wilderness area. (Source of data: USGS 2005 [National Atlas; http://nationalatlas.gov] and NPS)

Map J.   Park-specific map: Locations of high-elevation lakes within the principal park (GRSM) that occurs within this network. The method for designation as high elevation is explained in the text. (Source of data: U.S. EPA National Elevation Dataset and U.S. EPA/USGS National Hydrography Dataset Plus [http://www.horizon-systems.com/nhdplus/])

Map AT-C.   Total N emissions by county for lands surrounding the Appalachian Trail corridor, expressed as tons of N emitted into the atmosphere per square mile per year. The total includes both oxidized (nitrogen oxides, NO_x) and reduced (ammonia, NH_3) N. (Source of data: EPA National Emissions Inventory, http://www.epa.gov/ttn/chief/net/2002inventory.html)

Map AT-D.   Major point source emissions of oxidized (nitrogen oxides, NO_x) and reduced (ammonia, NH_3) N in and around the Appalachian Trail corridor. The base of each vertical bar is positioned in the map at the approximate location of the source. The height of the bar is proportional to the magnitude of the source. (Source of data: EPA National Emissions Inventory, http://www.epa.gov/ttn/chief/net/2002inventory.html)

Map AT-E.   Urban centers having more than 10,000 people near Appalachian Trail corridor and within a 300-mile buffer around the perimeter of the corridor. (Source of data: U.S. Census 2000)

Map AT-F.   Total N deposition in and around the Appalachian Trail corridor. Included in the total are wet plus dry forms of both oxidized (nitrogen oxides, NO_x) and reduced (ammonia, NH_3) N. Values are expressed as kilograms of N deposited per hectare per year. (Source of data: Interpolated NADP wet and CMAQ Model dry deposition (east of 70° longitude); data for 2002; see information for Map B above)

Map AT-G.   Land cover types in and around the Appalachian Trail corridor, based on the National Land Cover dataset. (Source of data: National Land Cover Dataset, http://www.mrlc.gov/nlcd_multizone_map.php)

Map AT-I.   Lands within and near the Appalachian Trail corridor that are classified as Class I or wilderness area. (Source of Data: USGS 2005 [National Atlas; http://nationalatlas.gov] and NPS)

Figure A.   Network rankings for Pollutant Exposure, calculated as the average of scores for all Pollutant Exposure variables.

Figure B.   Network rankings for Ecosystem Sensitivity, calculated as the average of scores for all Ecosystem Sensitivity variables.

Figure C.   Network rankings for Park Protection, calculated as the average of scores for all Park Protection variables.

Figure D.   Network Summary Risk ranking, calculated as the sum of the averages of the scores for Pollutant Exposure, Ecosystem Sensitivity, and Park Protection.

Figure E.   Park rankings for Pollutant Exposure for all parks larger than 100 square miles. Ranks for each park were calculated relative to all parks, regardless of size, as the average of scores for all Pollutant Exposure variables.

Figure F.   Park rankings for Ecosystem Sensitivity for all parks larger than 100 square miles. Ranks for each park were calculated relative to all parks, regardless of size, as the average of scores for all Ecosystem Sensitivity variables.

Figure G.   Park rankings for Park Protection for all parks larger than 100 square miles. Ranks for each park were calculated relative to all parks, regardless of size, as the average of scores for all Park Protection variables.

Figure H.   Park rankings for Summary Risk for all parks larger than 100 square miles. Ranks for each park were calculated relative to all parks, regardless of size, as the average of scores for all Summary Risk variables.

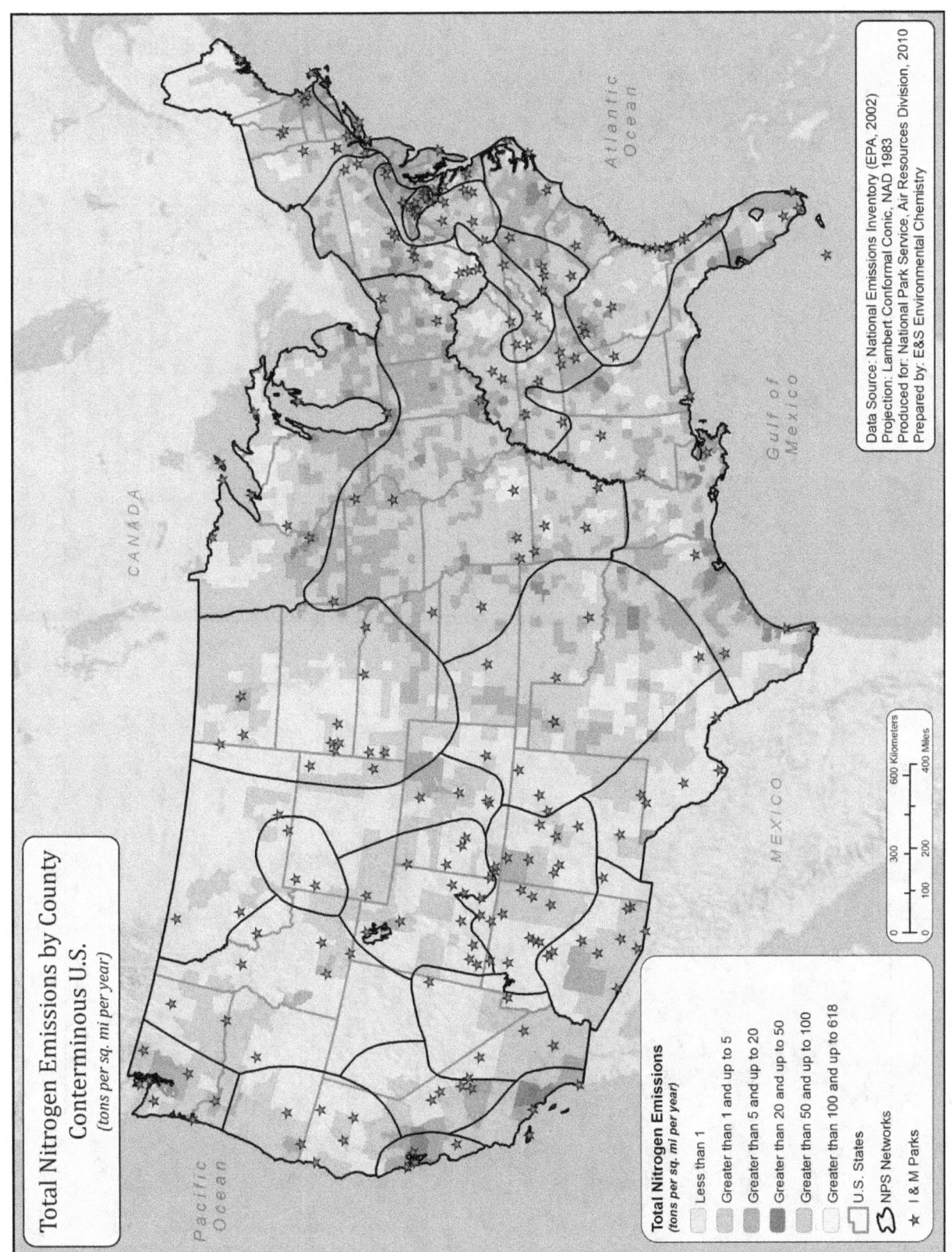

Total Nitrogen Emissions by County
Conterminous U.S.
(tons per sq. mi per year)

Total Nitrogen Emissions
(tons per sq. mi per year)

Less than 1
Greater than 1 and up to 5
Greater than 5 and up to 20
Greater than 20 and up to 50
Greater than 50 and up to 100
Greater than 100 and up to 618
U.S. States
NPS Networks
I & M Parks

Data Source: National Emissions Inventory (EPA, 2002)
Projection: Lambert Conformal Conic, NAD 1983
Produced for: National Park Service, Air Resources Division, 2010
Prepared by: E&S Environmental Chemistry

Map A

APHN-7

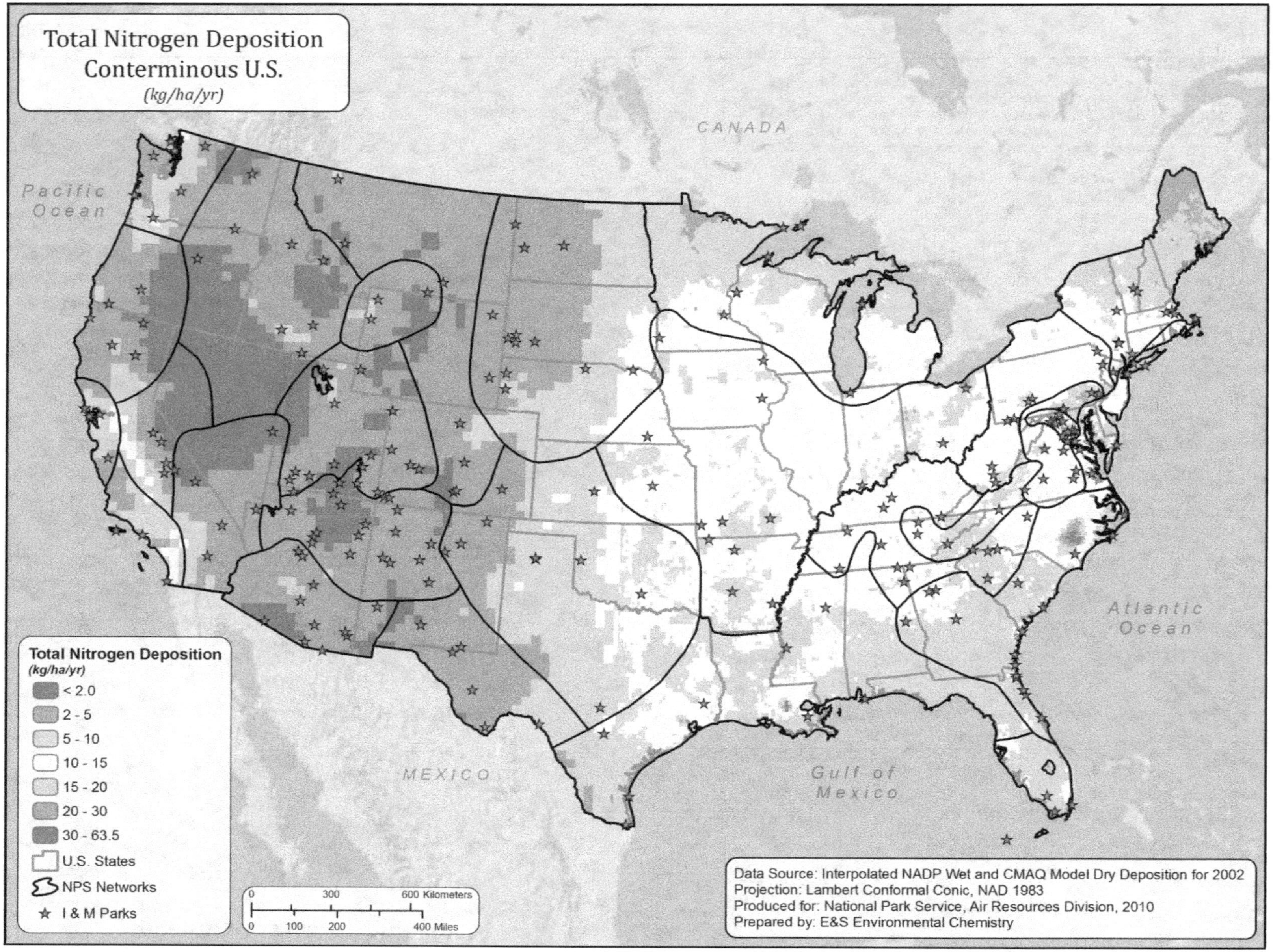

**Total Nitrogen Deposition
Conterminous U.S.**

(kg/ha/yr)

Total Nitrogen Deposition
(kg/ha/yr)
- < 2.0
- 2 - 5
- 5 - 10
- 10 - 15
- 15 - 20
- 20 - 30
- 30 - 63.5
- U.S. States
- ∿ NPS Networks
- ★ I & M Parks

CANADA

MEXICO

Pacific
Ocean

Atlantic
Ocean

Gulf of
Mexico

Data Source: Interpolated NADP Wet and CMAQ Model Dry Deposition for 2002
Projection: Lambert Conformal Conic, NAD 1983
Produced for: National Park Service, Air Resources Division, 2010
Prepared by: E&S Environmental Chemistry

0   100   200   300   600 Kilometers
0   200   400 Miles

Map B

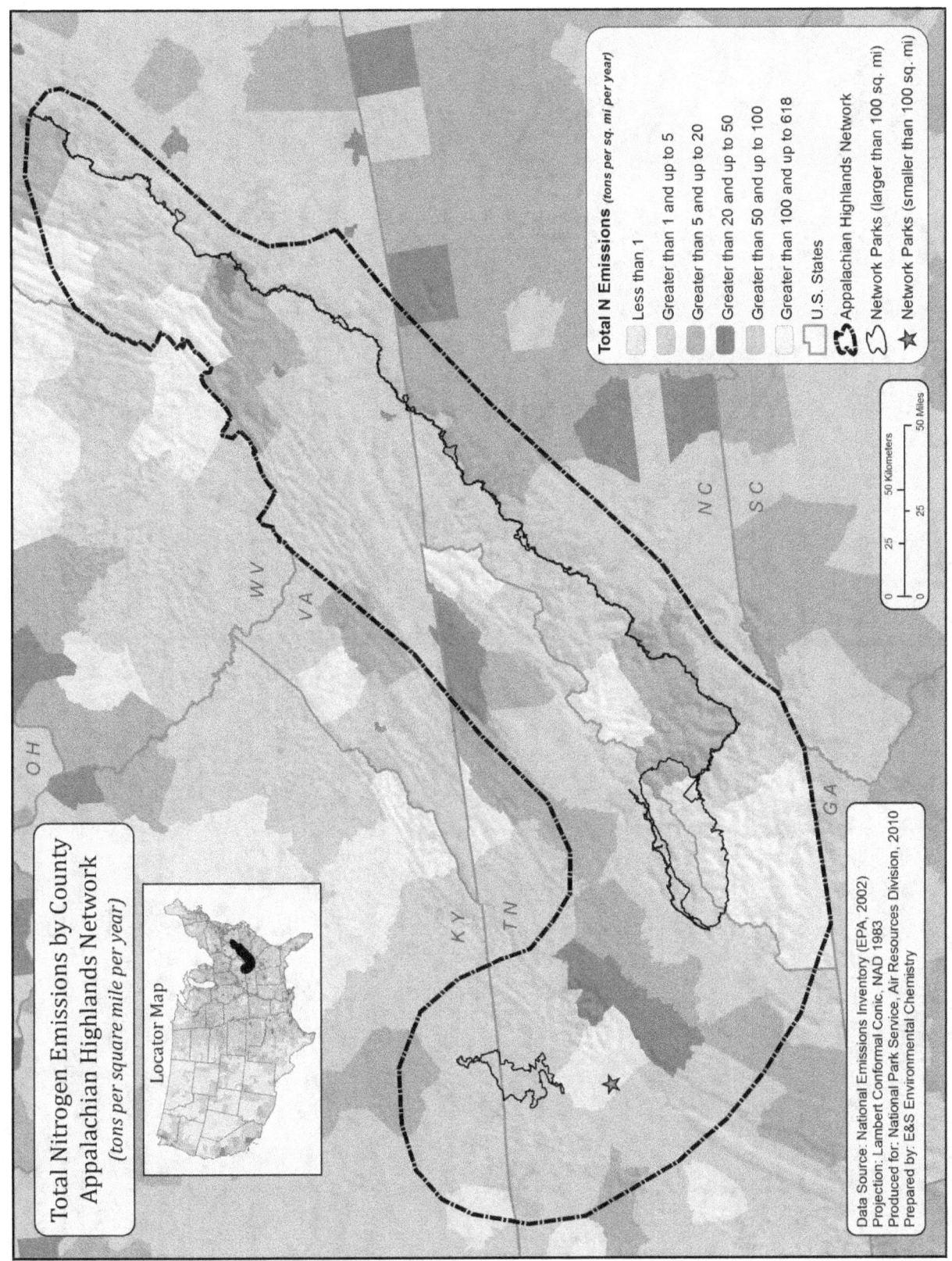

Total Nitrogen Emissions by County
Appalachian Highlands Network
(tons per square mile per year)

Locator Map

Total N Emissions *(tons per sq. mi per year)*

Less than 1
Greater than 1 and up to 5
Greater than 5 and up to 20
Greater than 20 and up to 50
Greater than 50 and up to 100
Greater than 100 and up to 618

U.S. States
Appalachian Highlands Network
Network Parks (larger than 100 sq. mi)
Network Parks (smaller than 100 sq. mi)

Data Source: National Emissions Inventory (EPA, 2002)
Projection: Lambert Conformal Conic, NAD 1983
Produced for: National Park Service, Air Resources Division, 2010
Prepared by: E&S Environmental Chemistry

O H
W V
V A
K Y
T N
N C
S C
G A

0   25   50 Kilometers
0   25   50 Miles

Map C

APHN-9

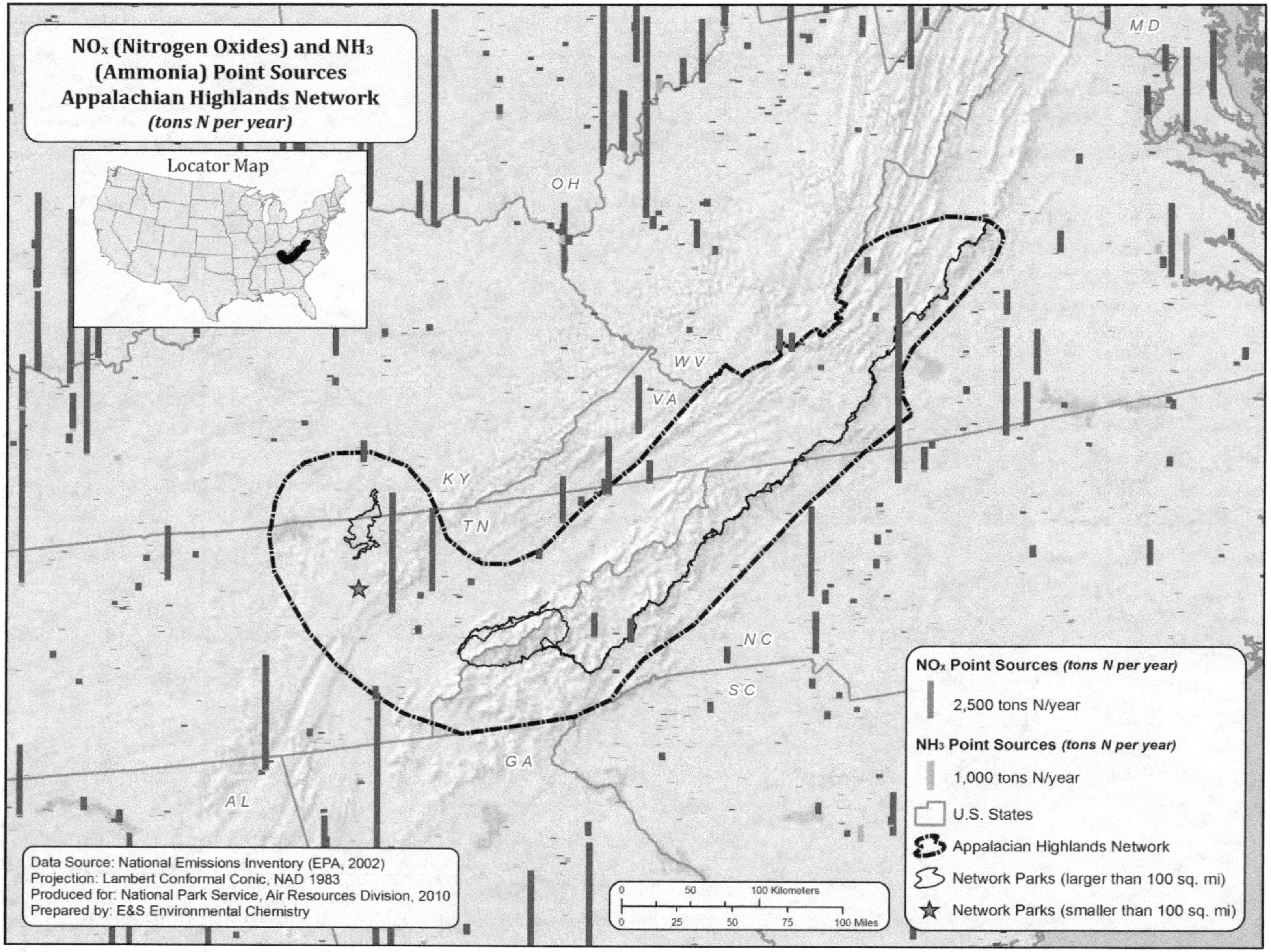

NOx (Nitrogen Oxides) and NH3 (Ammonia) Point Sources
Appalachian Highlands Network
(tons N per year)

Locator Map

NOx Point Sources *(tons N per year)*
━━━ 2,500 tons N/year

NH3 Point Sources *(tons N per year)*
━━━ 1,000 tons N/year

☐ U.S. States

Appalacian Highlands Network

Network Parks (larger than 100 sq. mi)

★ Network Parks (smaller than 100 sq. mi)

100 Kilometers
0   25   50   75   100 Miles

Data Source: National Emissions Inventory (EPA, 2002)
Projection: Lambert Conformal Conic, NAD 1983
Produced for: National Park Service, Air Resources Division, 2010
Prepared by: E&S Environmental Chemistry

Map D

APHN-10

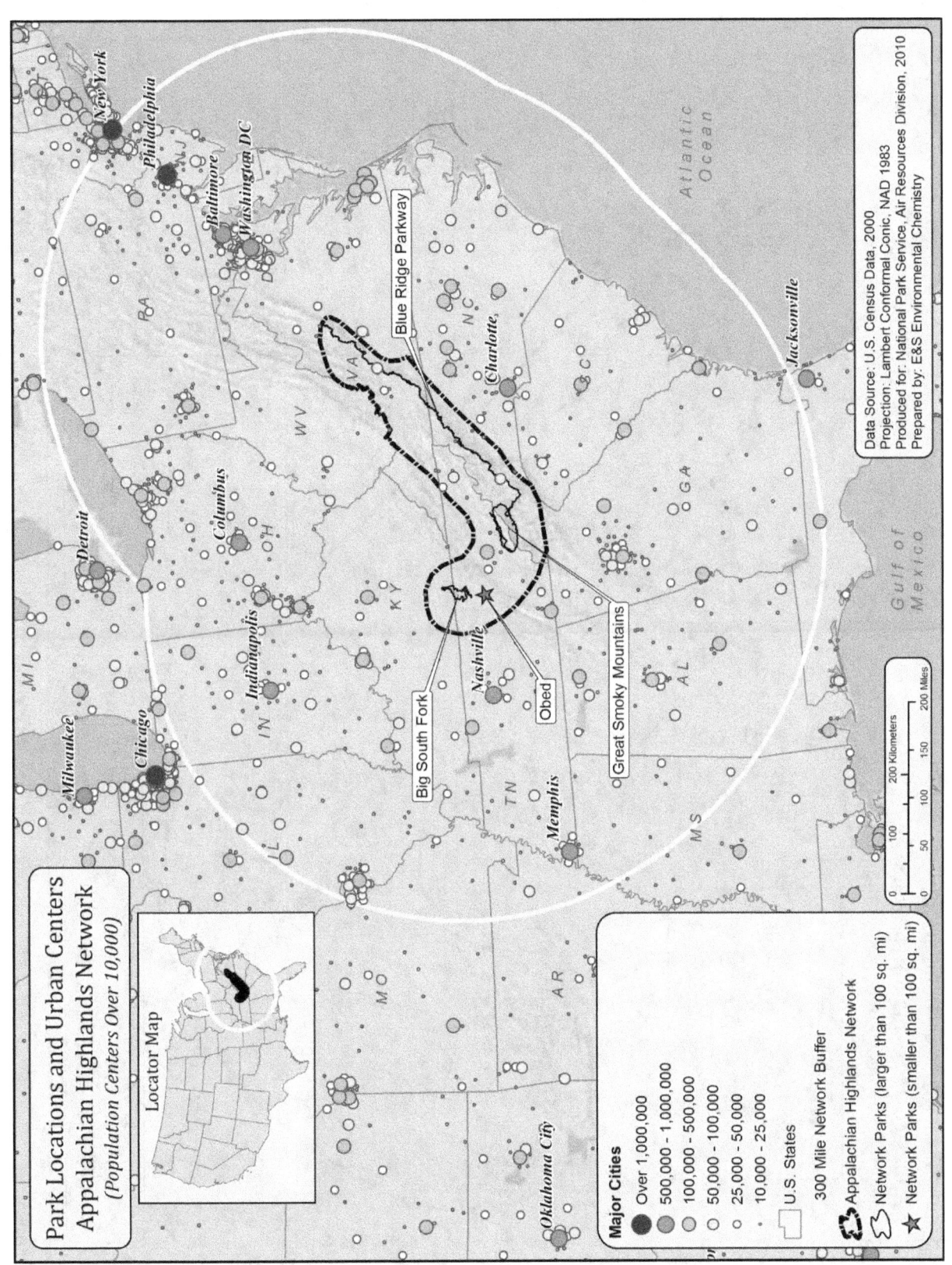

Park Locations and Urban Centers
Appalachian Highlands Network
(Population Centers Over 10,000)

Locator Map

Major Cities
- ⬤ Over 1,000,000
- ⬤ 500,000 - 1,000,000
- ⬤ 100,000 - 500,000
- ◯ 50,000 - 100,000
- ◯ 25,000 - 50,000
- · 10,000 - 25,000
- ▢ U.S. States
- 300 Mile Network Buffer
- ⬠ Appalachian Highlands Network
- ⬠ Network Parks (larger than 100 sq. mi)
- ★ Network Parks (smaller than 100 sq. mi)

Blue Ridge Parkway

Big South Fork

Nashville

Obed

Great Smoky Mountains

New York
Philadelphia
Baltimore
Washington DC
Jacksonville
Charlotte
Columbus
Detroit
Indianapolis
Chicago
Milwaukee
Memphis
Oklahoma City

Atlantic Ocean
Gulf of Mexico

PA
WV
VA
NC
SC
GA
OH
KY
TN
AL
MS
IN
IL
MI
AR
MO

Data Source: U.S. Census Data, 2000
Projection: Lambert Conformal Conic, NAD 1983
Produced for: National Park Service, Air Resources Division, 2010
Prepared by: E&S Environmental Chemistry

0   50   100   200 Kilometers
0   50   100   150   200 Miles

Map E

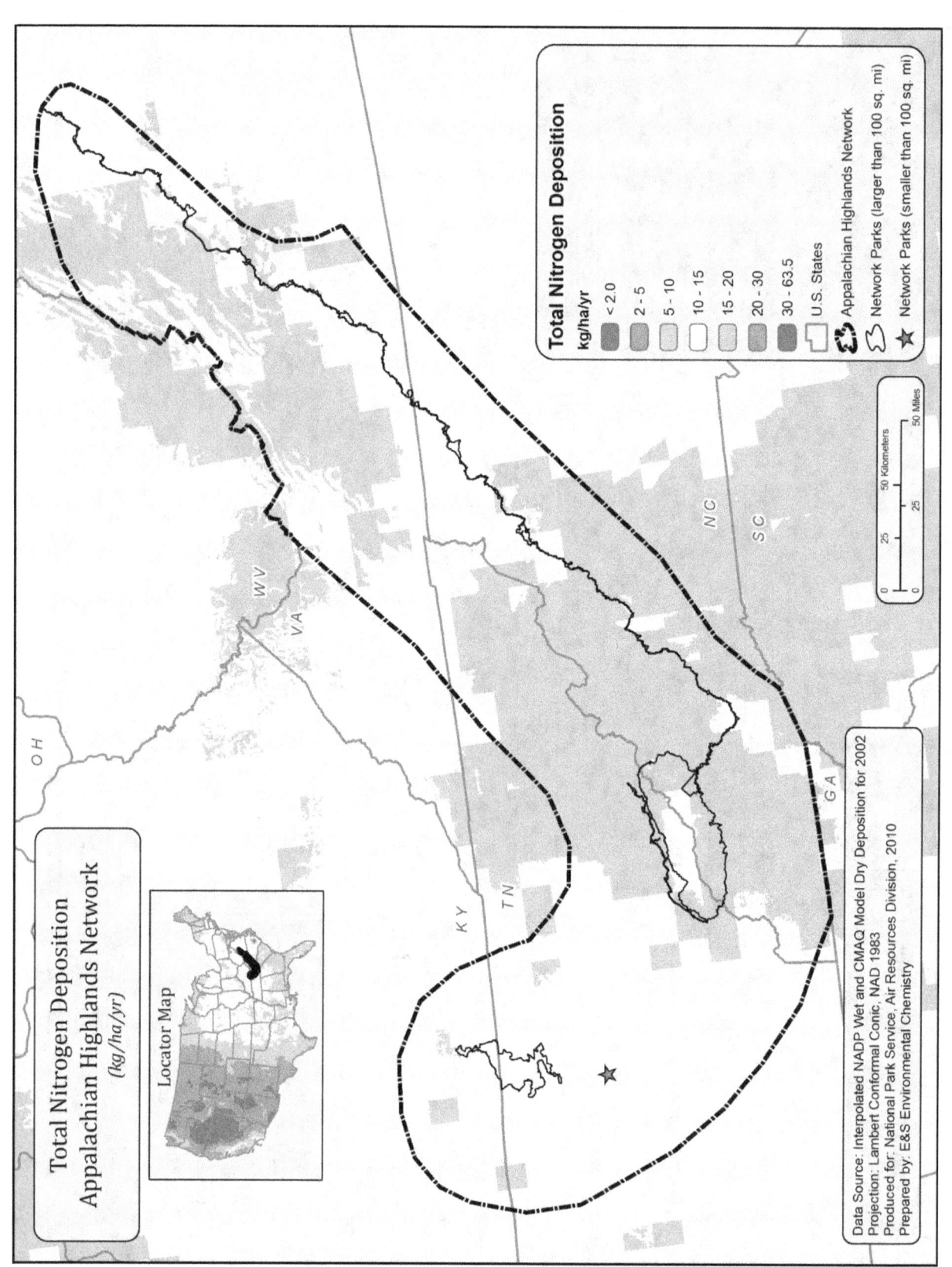

Total Nitrogen Deposition
Appalachian Highlands Network
(kg/ha/yr)

Locator Map

Total Nitrogen Deposition

kg/ha/yr

- < 2.0
- 2 - 5
- 5 - 10
- 10 - 15
- 15 - 20
- 20 - 30
- 30 - 63.5
- U.S. States

Appalachian Highlands Network

Network Parks (larger than 100 sq. mi)

Network Parks (smaller than 100 sq. mi)

0 25 50 Kilometers
0 25 50 Miles

OH

WV

VA

KY

TN

NC

SC

GA

Data Source: Interpolated NADP Wet and CMAQ Model Dry Deposition for 2002
Projection: Lambert Conformal Conic, NAD 1983
Produced for: National Park Service, Air Resources Division, 2010
Prepared by: E&S Environmental Chemistry

Map F

APHN-12

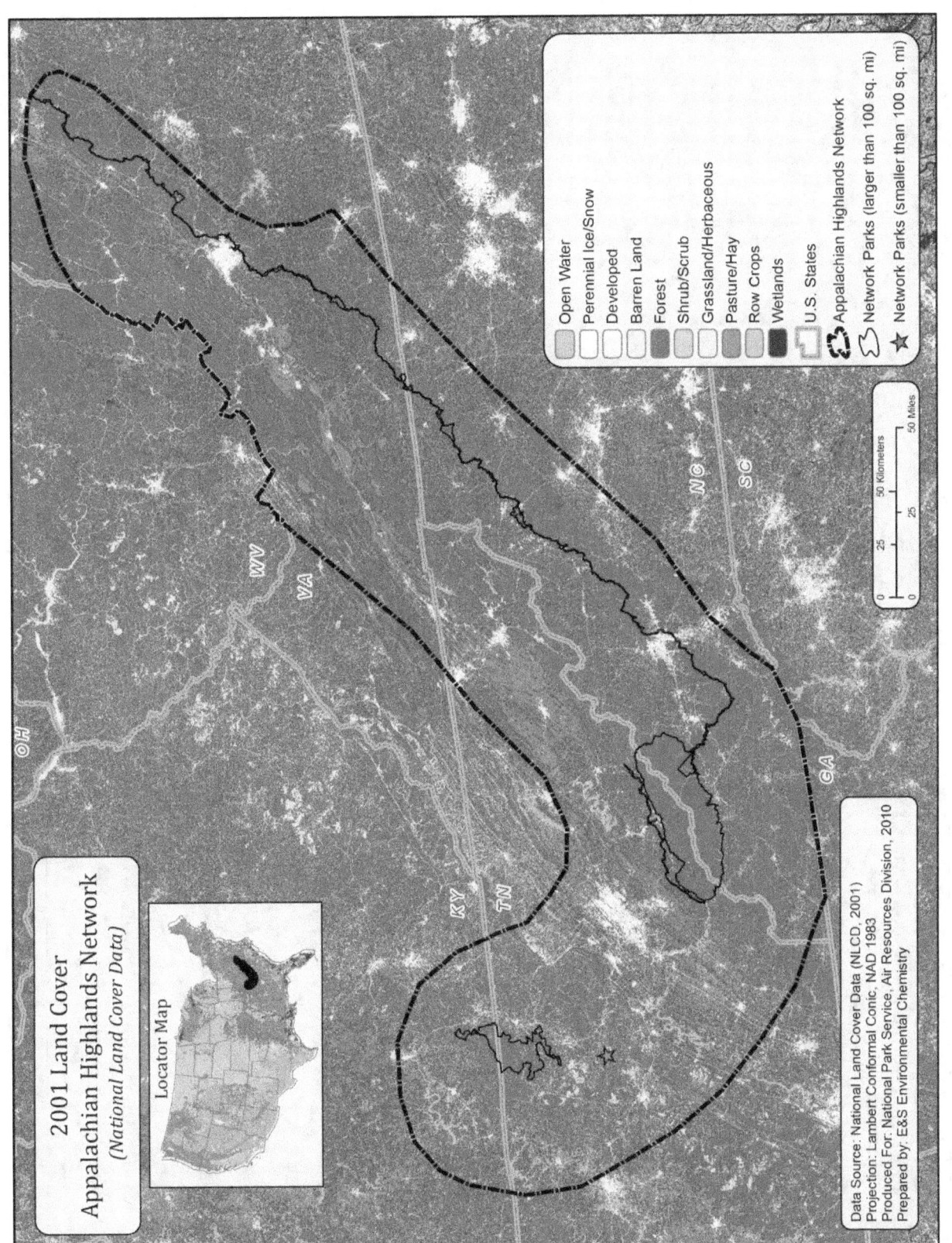

2001 Land Cover
Appalachian Highlands Network
(National Land Cover Data)

Locator Map

Legend

Open Water
Perennial Ice/Snow
Developed
Barren Land
Forest
Shrub/Scrub
Grassland/Herbaceous
Pasture/Hay
Row Crops
Wetlands
U.S. States
Appalachian Highlands Network
Network Parks (larger than 100 sq. mi)
Network Parks (smaller than 100 sq. mi)

OH
WV
VA
KY
TN
NC
SC
GA

0   25   50 Kilometers
0   25   50 Miles

Data Source: National Land Cover Data (NLCD, 2001)
Projection: Lambert Conformal Conic, NAD 1983
Produced For: National Park Service, Air Resources Division, 2010
Prepared by: E&S Environmental Chemistry

Map G

APHN-13

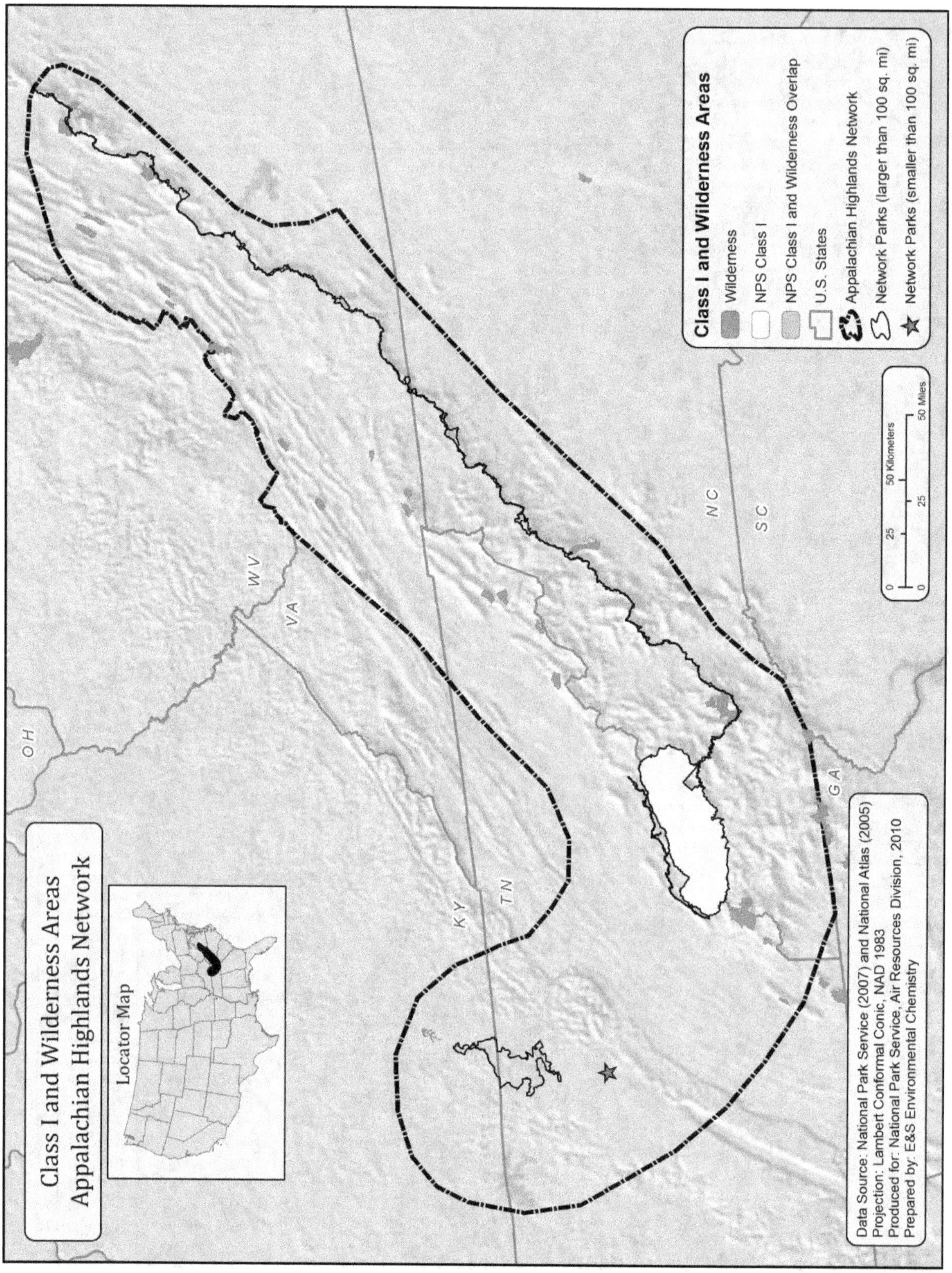

Class I and Wilderness Areas
Appalachian Highlands Network

Locator Map

Class I and Wilderness Areas

- Wilderness
- NPS Class I
- NPS Class I and Wilderness Overlap
- U.S. States
- Appalachian Highlands Network
- Network Parks (larger than 100 sq. mi)
- ★ Network Parks (smaller than 100 sq. mi)

0   25   50 Kilometers
0   25   50 Miles

Data Source: National Park Service (2007) and National Atlas (2005)
Projection: Lambert Conformal Conic, NAD 1983
Produced for: National Park Service, Air Resources Division, 2010
Prepared by: E&S Environmental Chemistry

Map I

OH
WV
VA
KY
TN
NC
SC
GA

APHN-14

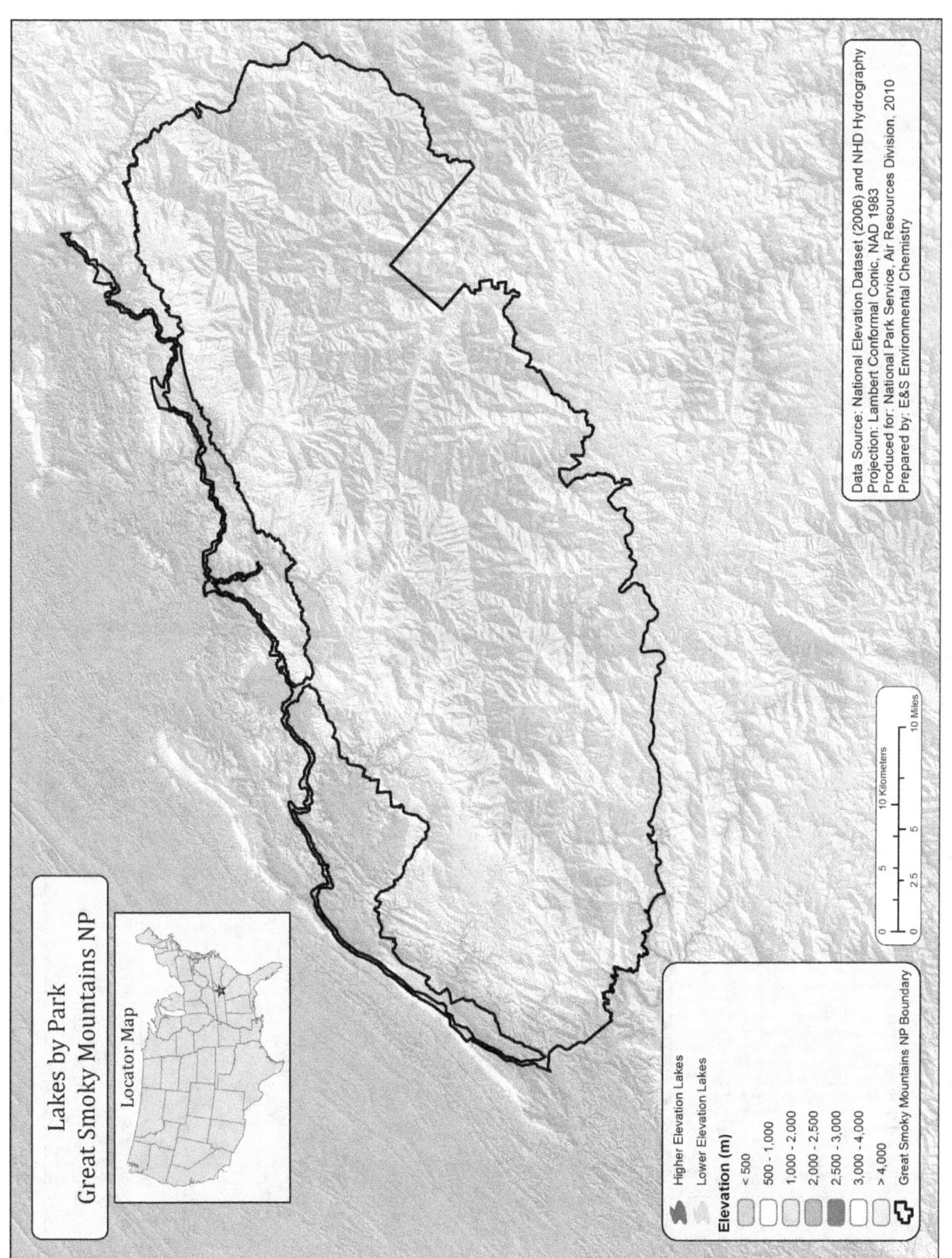

Lakes by Park
Great Smoky Mountains NP

Locator Map

Data Source: National Elevation Dataset (2006) and NHD Hydrography
Projection: Lambert Conformal Conic, NAD 1983
Produced for: National Park Service, Air Resources Division, 2010
Prepared by: E&S Environmental Chemistry

Higher Elevation Lakes
Lower Elevation Lakes

Elevation (m)
< 500
500 - 1,000
1,000 - 2,000
2,000 - 2,500
2,500 - 3,000
3,000 - 4,000
> 4,000

Great Smoky Mountains NP Boundary

0   5   10 Kilometers
0   2.5   5   10 Miles

Map J

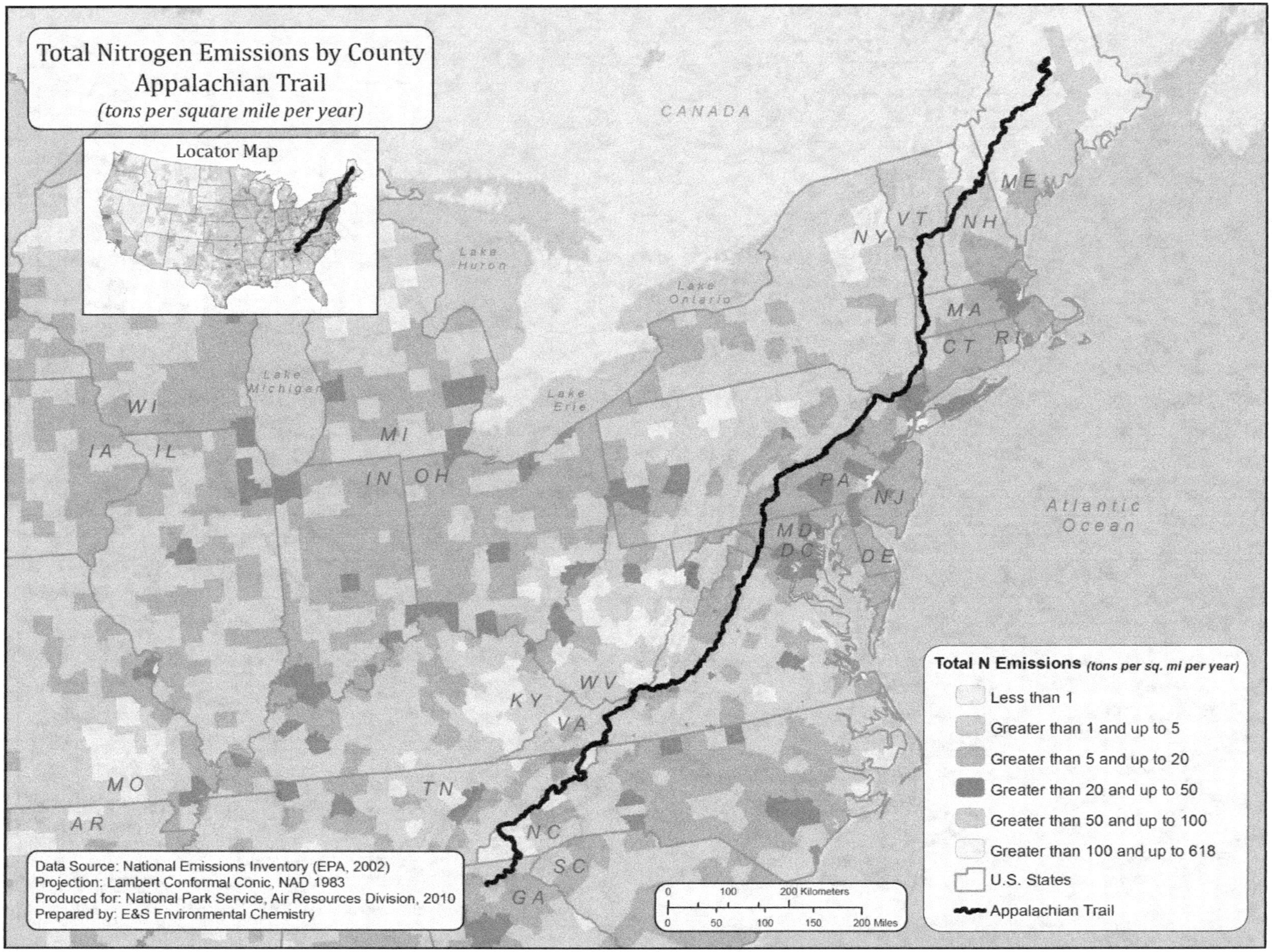

Total Nitrogen Emissions by County
Appalachian Trail
(tons per square mile per year)
Locator Map
CANADA
Lake Huron
Lake Ontario
Lake Michigan
Lake Erie
Atlantic Ocean
ME
NH
VT
NY
MA
CT
RI
PA
NJ
MD
DC
DE
WV
VA
KY
TN
NC
SC
GA
MI
IN
OH
WI
IA
IL
MO
AR
Total N Emissions (tons per sq. mi per year)
Less than 1
Greater than 1 and up to 5
Greater than 5 and up to 20
Greater than 20 and up to 50
Greater than 50 and up to 100
Greater than 100 and up to 618
U.S. States
Appalachian Trail
0 100 200 Kilometers
0 50 100 150 200 Miles
Data Source: National Emissions Inventory (EPA, 2002)
Projection: Lambert Conformal Conic, NAD 1983
Produced for: National Park Service, Air Resources Division, 2010
Prepared by: E&S Environmental Chemistry

Map AT-C

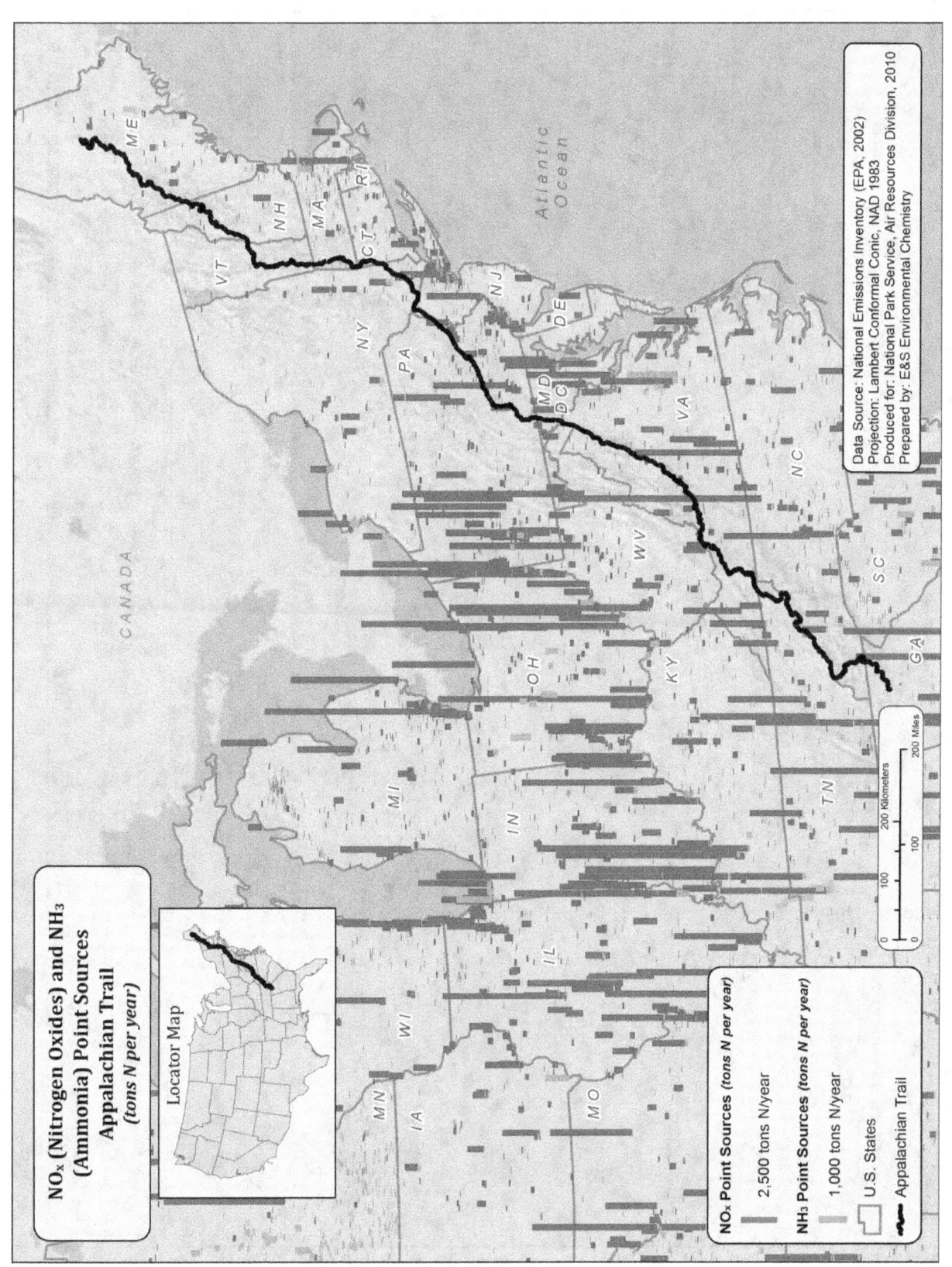

NO_x (Nitrogen Oxides) and NH_3 (Ammonia) Point Sources
Appalachian Trail
(tons N per year)

Locator Map

NO_x Point Sources (tons N per year)
▬ 2,500 tons N/year

NH_3 Point Sources (tons N per year)
▬ 1,000 tons N/year

☐ U.S. States

▬ Appalachian Trail

Data Source: National Emissions Inventory (EPA, 2002)
Projection: Lambert Conformal Conic, NAD 1983
Produced for: National Park Service, Air Resources Division, 2010
Prepared by: E&S Environmental Chemistry

Atlantic Ocean

CANADA

ME
NH
VT
MA
CT
RI
NY
NJ
PA
DE
MD
DC
VA
WV
NC
SC
KY
OH
IN
IL
TN
MI
WI
MN
IA
MO
GA

0 100 200 Kilometers
0 100 200 Miles

Map AT-D

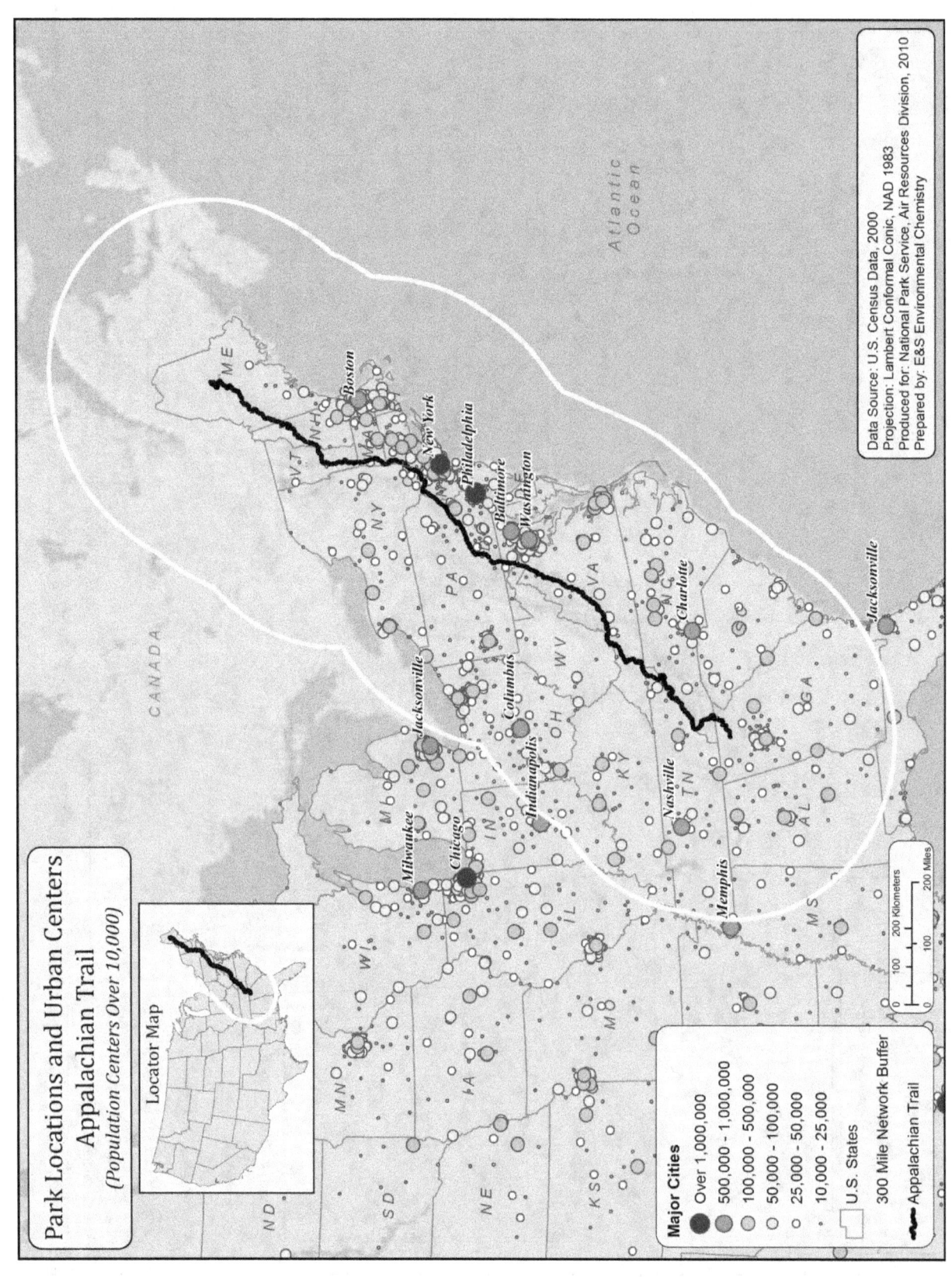

Park Locations and Urban Centers
Appalachian Trail
(Population Centers Over 10,000)

Locator Map

Atlantic Ocean

CANADA

Boston
New York
Philadelphia
Baltimore
Washington
Charlotte
Jacksonville
Jacksonville
Columbus
Milwaukee
Chicago
Indianapolis
Nashville
Memphis

ME
N.H.
VT.
MA
N.Y.
PA.
OH
WV
VA
N C
S C
GA
KY
TN
AL
MS
IN
IL
MO
IA
WI
MN
ND
SD
NE
KSO

Major Cities
- Over 1,000,000
- 500,000 - 1,000,000
- 100,000 - 500,000
- 50,000 - 100,000
- 25,000 - 50,000
- 10,000 - 25,000
- U.S. States
- 300 Mile Network Buffer
- Appalachian Trail

0   100   200 Kilometers
0   100   200 Miles

Data Source: U.S. Census Data, 2000
Projection: Lambert Conformal Conic, NAD 1983
Produced for: National Park Service, Air Resources Division, 2010
Prepared by: E&S Environmental Chemistry

Map AT-E

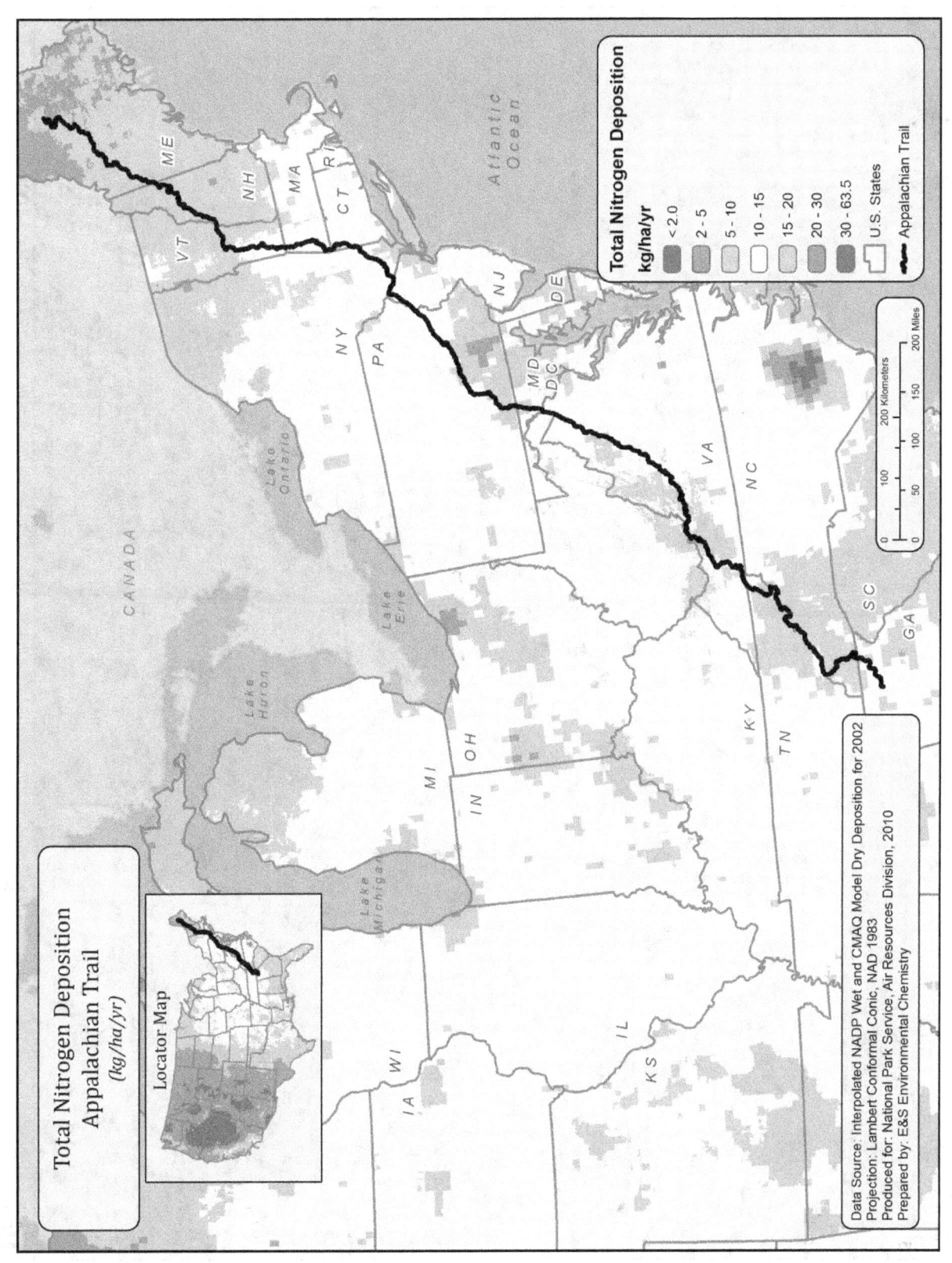

Total Nitrogen Deposition
Appalachian Trail
(kg/ha/yr)

Locator Map

Total Nitrogen Deposition

kg/ha/yr
- < 2.0
- 2 - 5
- 5 - 10
- 10 - 15
- 15 - 20
- 20 - 30
- 30 - 63.5

U.S. States

Appalachian Trail

Data Source: Interpolated NADP Wet and CMAQ Model Dry Deposition for 2002
Projection: Lambert Conformal Conic, NAD 1983
Produced for: National Park Service, Air Resources Division, 2010
Prepared by: E&S Environmental Chemistry

Map AT-F

2001 Land Cover
Appalachian Trail
(National Land Cover Data)

Locator Map

Legend
- Open Water
- Perennial Ice/Snow
- Developed
- Barren Land
- Forest
- Shrub/Scrub
- Grassland/Herbaceous
- Pasture/Hay
- Row Crops
- Wetlands
- U.S. States
- Appalachian Trail

Atlantic Ocean

CANADA

Lake Ontario
Lake Erie
Lake Huron
Lake Michigan

ME, NH, VT, MA, RI, CT, NY, PA, NJ, DE, MD, D.C., VA, NC, SC, GA, TN, KY, OH, MI, IN, IL, KS, WI, IA

0   100   200 Kilometers
0   50   100   150   200 Miles

Data Source: National Land Cover Data (NLCD 2001)
Projection: Lambert Conformal Conic, NAD 1983
Produced for: National Park Service, Air Resources Division, 2010
Prepared by: E&S Environmental Chemistry

Map AT-G

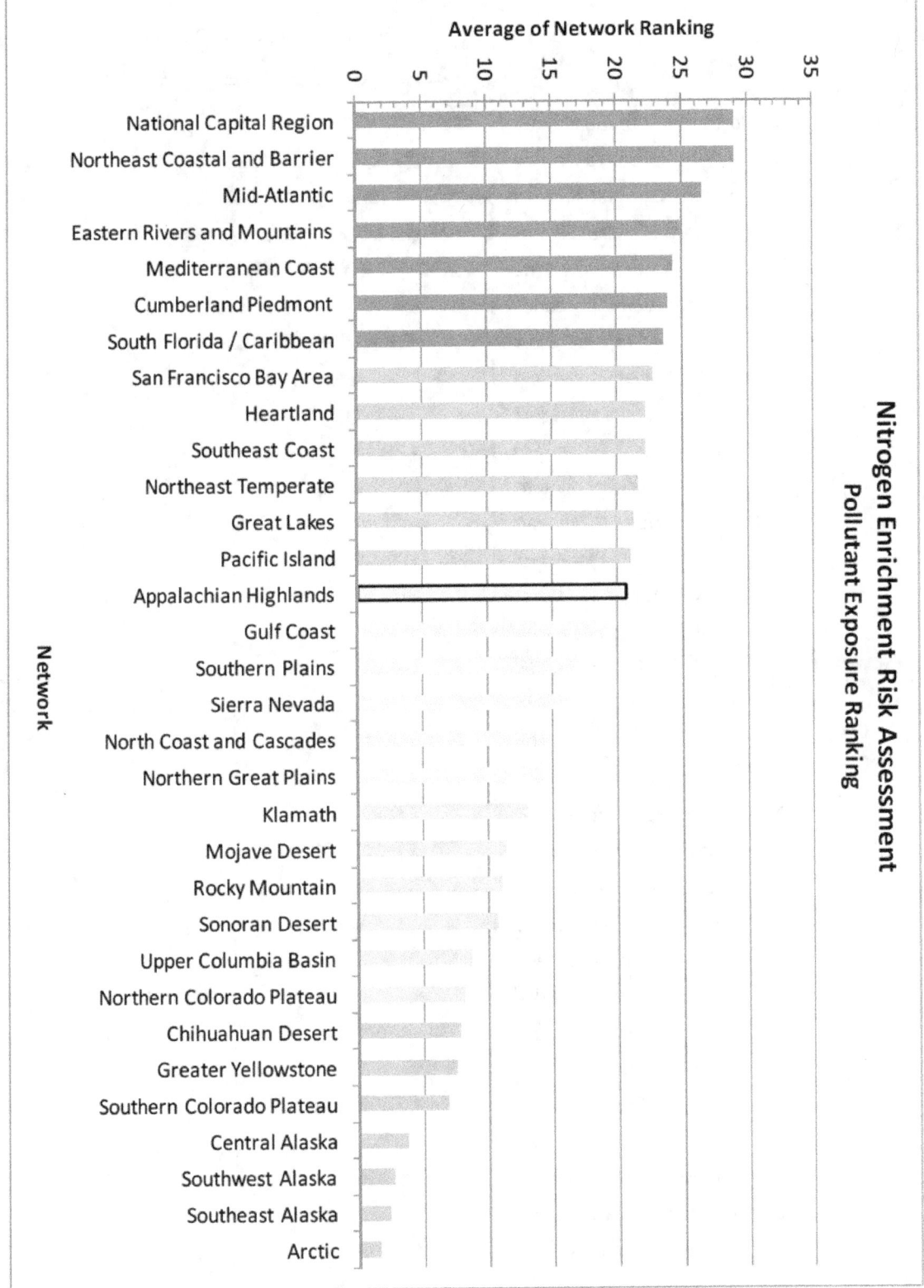

Figure A

Nitrogen Enrichment Risk Assessment
Pollutant Exposure Ranking

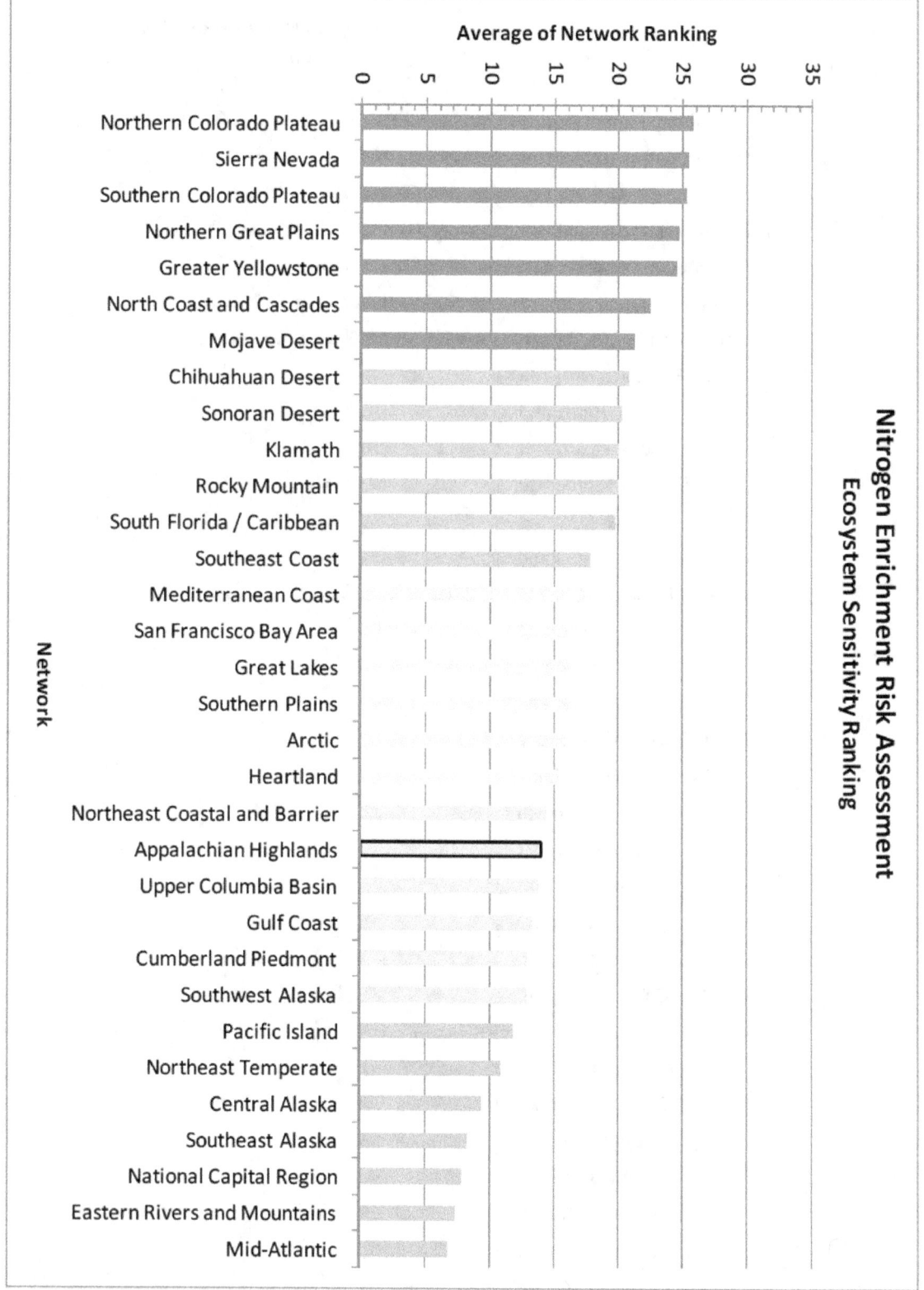

Figure B

Nitrogen Enrichment Risk Assessment
Ecosystem Sensitivity Ranking

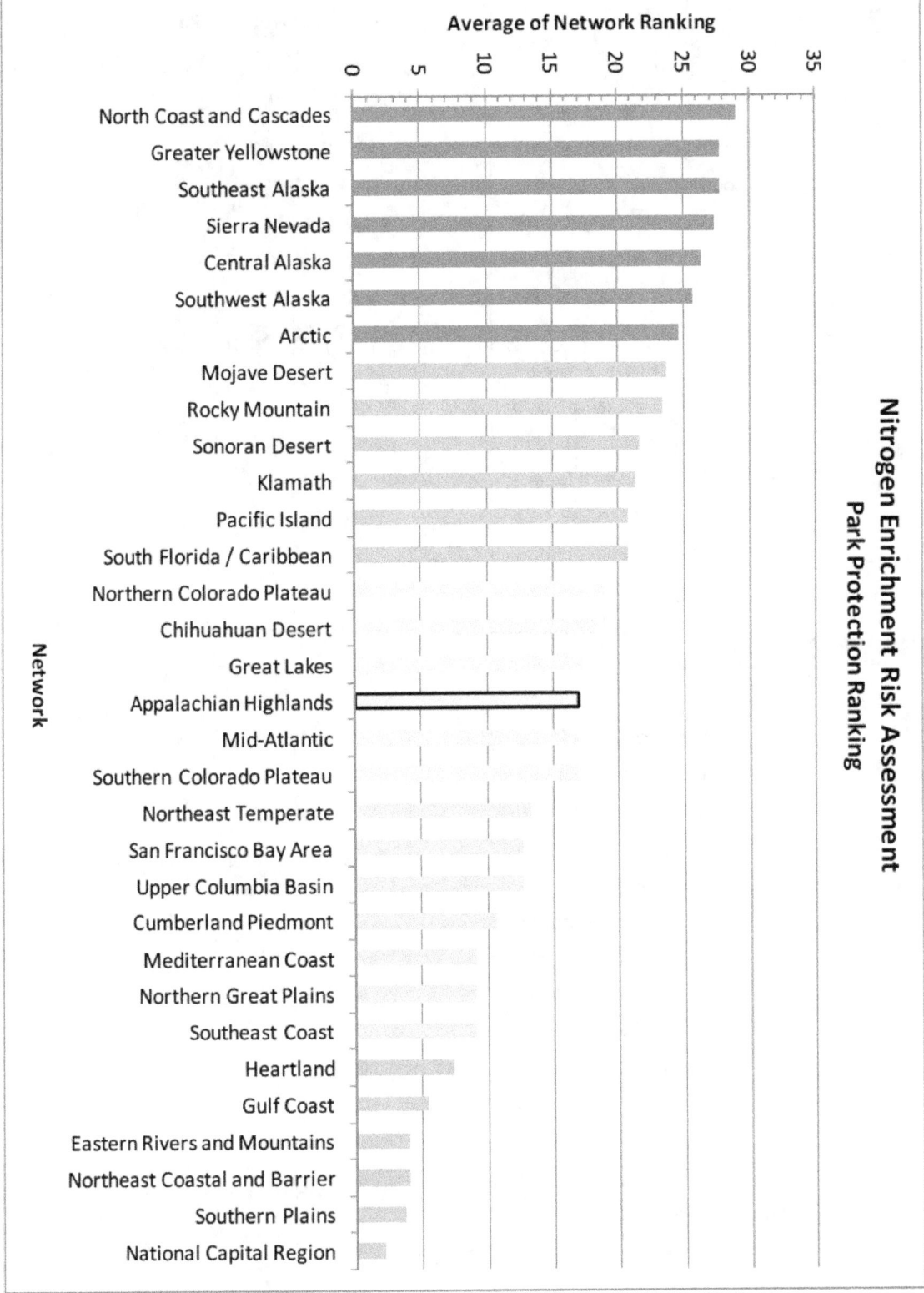

Figure C

Nitrogen Enrichment Risk Assessment
Park Protection Ranking

Figure D

Nitrogen Enrichment Risk Assessment
Summary Risk Ranking

Nitrogen Enrichment Risk Assessment

Appalachian Highlands Network - Pollutant Exposure Ranking

Figure E

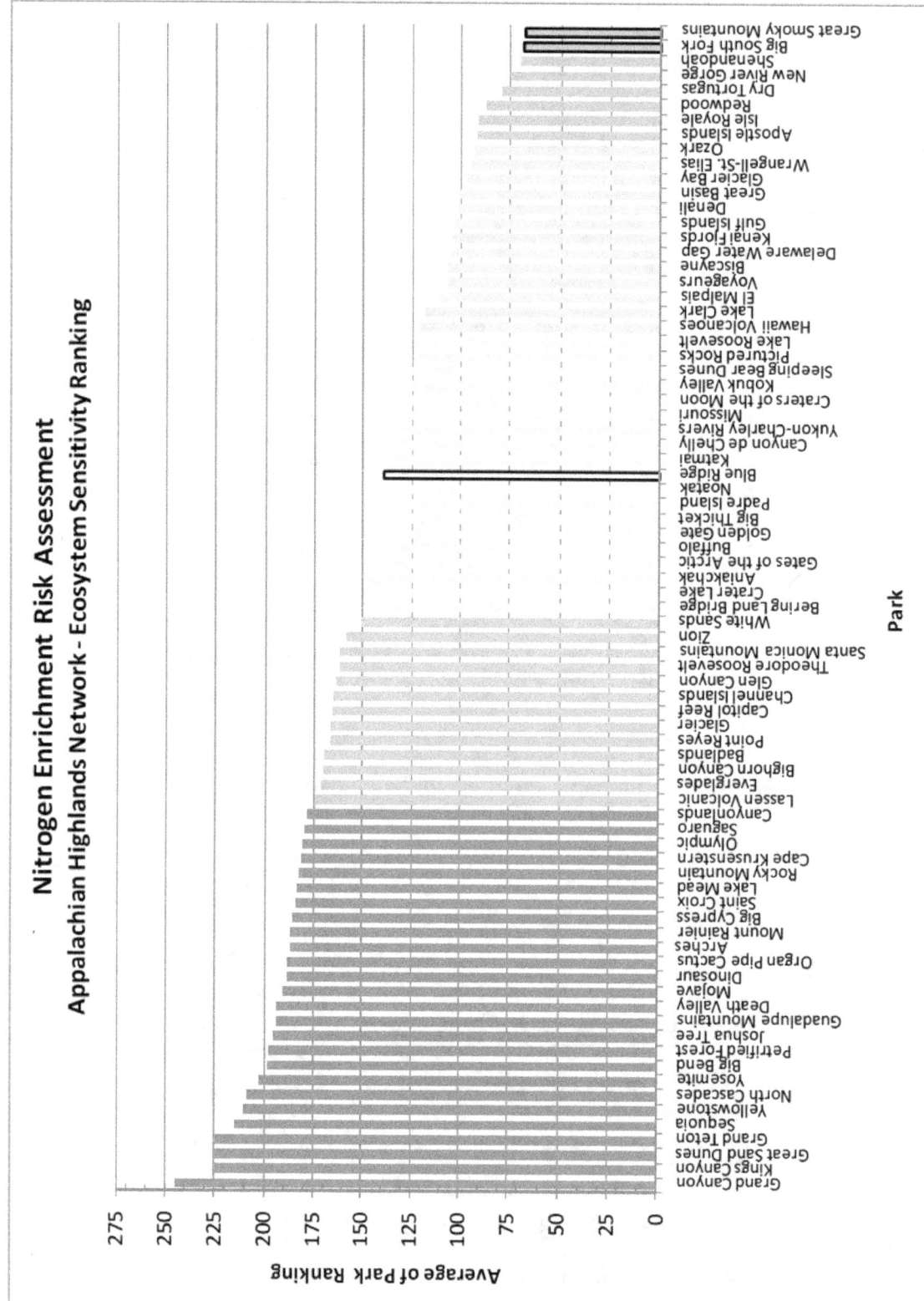

Figure F

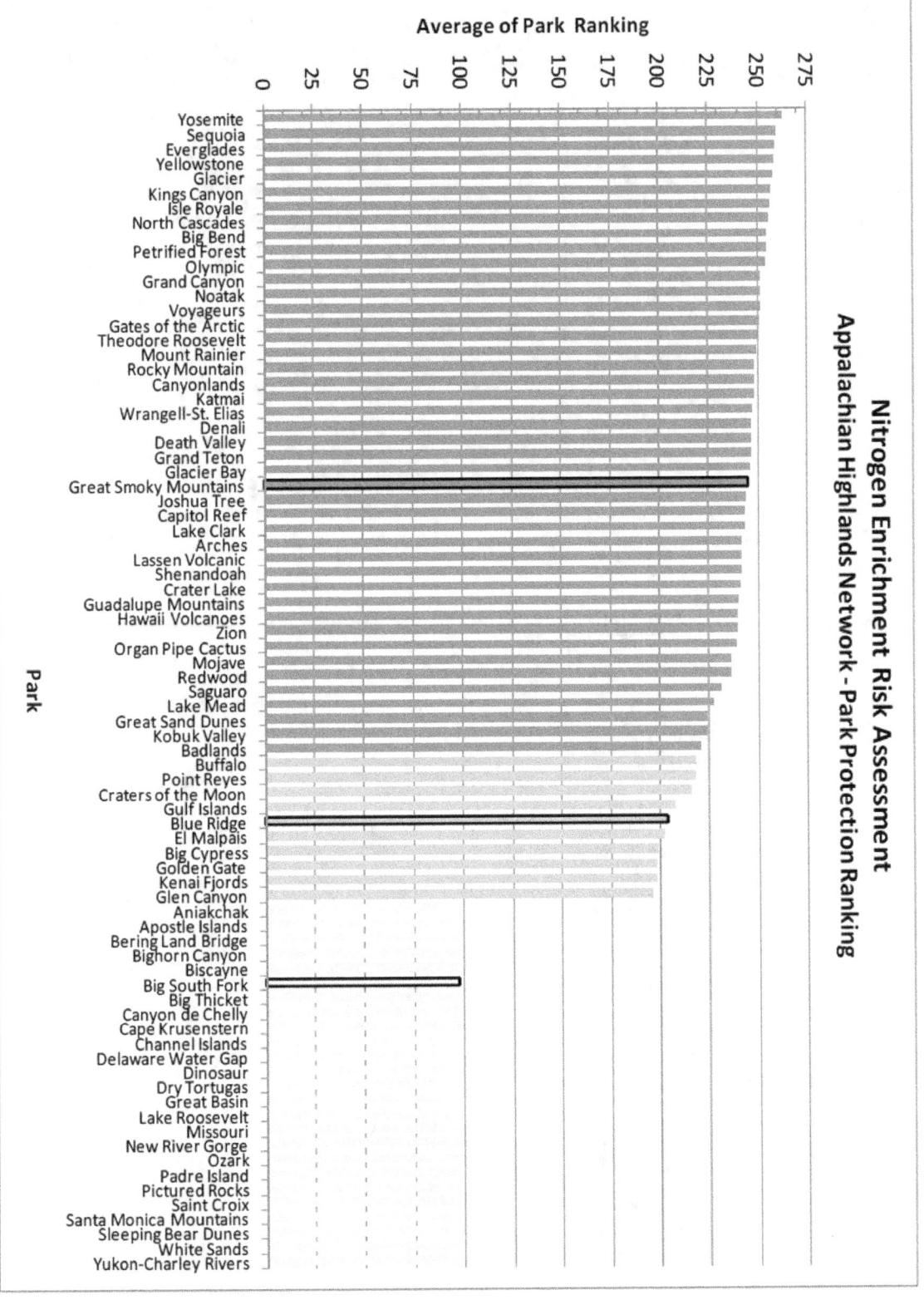

Figure G

Nitrogen Enrichment Risk Assessment
Appalachian Highlands Network - Park Protection Ranking

Nitrogen Enrichment Risk Assessment
Appalachian Highlands Network - Summary Risk Ranking

Average of Park Ranking

275 | 250 | 225 | 200 | 175 | 150 | 125 | 100 | 75 | 50 | 25 | 0

Park:
Everglades, Sequoia, North Cascades, Yosemite, Joshua Tree, Kings Canyon, Mount Rainier, Olympic, Point Reyes, Big Cypress, Rocky Mountain, Grand Canyon, Grand Teton, Mojave, Yellowstone, Blue Ridge, Shenandoah, Petrified Forest, Buffalo, Golden Gate, Death Valley, Guadalupe Mountains, Theodore Roosevelt, Saguaro, Organ Pipe Cactus, Great Sand Dunes, Glacier, Lassen Volcanic, Big Bend, Great Smoky Mountains, Crater Lake, Gulf Islands, Lake Mead, Arches, Canyonlands, Voyageurs, Santa Monica Mountains, Capitol Reef, Zion, Badlands, Saint Croix, Big Thicket, Delaware Water Gap, Isle Royale, Hawaii Volcanoes, Redwood, Gates of the Arctic, Craters of the Moon, Channel Islands, Noatak, Glen Canyon, Katmai, Missouri, Biscayne, Padre Island, Lake Clark, El Malpais, Denali, Kobuk Valley, Sleeping Bear Dunes, Wrangell-St. Elias, Glacier Bay, New River Gorge, Ozark, Pictured Rocks, Dinosaur, Big South Fork, Kenai Fjords, Bighorn Canyon, Canyon de Chelly, Cape Krusenstern, Apostle Islands, White Sands, Dry Tortugas, Lake Roosevelt, Bering Land Bridge, Yukon-Charley Rivers, Aniakchak, Great Basin

Figure H

NPS 910/106632, February 2011